4 Ways To Milk Money Off The Internet:

Powerful ways to use the Internet to Milk Money for Yourself

By Paul Marden

All rights reserved. No part of this publication may be reproduced, distributed, or transmitted in any form or by any means, including photocopying, recording, or other electronic or mechanical methods, without the prior written permission of the publisher, except in the case of brief quotations embodied in critical reviews and certain other noncommercial uses permitted by copyright law.

Copyright © Paul Marden, 2022.

Table of content

Chapter 1

Chapter 2

Chapter 3

Chapter 4

Chapter 1
4 Ways to use the Internet to Milk Money for Yourself

Hello [(Your name)], I'm glad you have received this book from me. I am Paul Marden. I am revealing systems I have used to create multiple figures of cash and assets for myself and millions of people like you. You are no different from me, meaning you can achieve even 10X what people have done with these systems. But you have to make a promise to me which is that you do not share these systems with un-serious people.

These systems have proven to work after having a productive mindset, with a consistent and relentless approach. An Unserious person cannot take advantage of this opportunity. If you are un-serious, the opportunities in this E-book cannot work for you. You could as well stop reading and save your time for the next un-serious thing on your mind and come back when you're ready.

If you have these things I've mentioned above, then I am going to say this, The contents of this book will change your life, and way of thinking, and transform you into a new. Stick with me and let's get the party started.

The internet today is a powerful tool in today's world, What I'm about to show you is an opportunity where you can make use of the internet in the marketing space to make income for yourself not by gambling on your choices but by learning high digital skills and applying this in the marketing ecosystem.

What I want to show you is a legitimate source of making money which is called affiliate marketing. You might be thinking that this is another form of referral business or one in which you have to bring people in for you to make money, rather this is a model where you learn quality digital skills that mold you for any financial sector you might venture into. Therefore, Ladies and Gentlemen, I present to you, the 72IG in means the 72 Hour Income Generator. This is a program that trains you on 10 high-income skills and free templates have generated millions for people who are no different from you meaning you can copy and paste what's already working for them. You get to learn Twitter Marketing,

WhatsApp marketing, Facebook ads IG ads, Content marketing Copywriting, Email Marketing, Sales funnel design, Graphics design, and Web design. This 72IG also gives you access to a paid account for free for a year where you can make 30%-80% in commissions by affiliating digital products. The amazing thing is that with these skills you can use them to promote your business or use them as a service to other people and charge them as a freelancer Or you can also use this to sell the products in your free affiliate account that you'll get through this same 72IG course you could do both still, depending on you! So if you sell a product of $120 with a $60 commission 10 times. That means you've made $600 right? You'll therefore be getting Twitter marketing worth $50.1 WhatsApp marketing worth $30 Facebook ads worth $50 IG ads worth $100 Content marketing worth $100 Copywriting worth $100 Email marketing worth $70 Sales funnel design worth $200 Graphics design worth $200 Web design worth $200 Plus free templates that have generated millions for people's businesses worth $601, you even get access to the weekly online classes from experts in this business.

The 72IG was once $80 then got to $90 then $100 and currently $124 only!! because of the opportunity has provided. This offer is only available for a short period as the price for the 72IG will soon increase to $150 because of its worth.

This can take you from zero to the top so see this as an investment in yourself that would yield financial freedom and cash flow.

Another Opportunity you can use to milk money using the internet is a Digital skill called Copywriting. This is a very hot skill that has converted millions of people like you and that is why I have decided to put this in this E-book.

Maximizing profit through Copywriting; Story of Stevens

Copywriting is the occupation of writing a piece of text for an advertisement or publicity material. Yes, occupation in the sense that you can make money off copywriting and writing as a full-time career or job.

Not surprisingly, creative writing is most commonly considered an art form. The creative arc of a plotline and narrative voice draws a natural link between this pleasurable pastime and the art world while it's easy to see the art in creative writing.

"Even if you've never been paid to write before, Even if your English is 'Poor', Even

if you struggled in School, Even if those around you don't believe you'll ever amount to anything in life..."

With no writing experience, people have gone from zero to $1000 to $10,000 and more from writing. This is a digital skill that up your game in every facet of life I will mention a few which are: Engineering, Science, Information Technology, Business, Sales, Travel, Space, and Astrology.

Now, you must be wondering what you need to do to benefit from the writing industry, before I get into that, I want to unfold the enormous value gotten from writing after a couple of months with Toyin Omotoso by telling you a little story.

This is Stevens, a young black boy from Lagos, Nigeria who grew up with struggling parents who had to sacrifice a lot to provide for his basic needs.

Due to this, Stevens lacked a lot of things growing up as a child and was deprived of basic things such as electricity, clothes, water, a good smartphone (neither did he have a bad one), internet access, and lots more.

This was a huge setback for Stevens as his peers in the outside world had even more at their comfort.

He struggled to finish his junior-level exams at a local high school where he dropped out from cause his parents could no longer provide these basic things for him, rather he joined in putting work in the family fishing where he would follow his father with a fishing hook and line, casting it into the water, while his mother would get the fish gotten and smoke it for sale. This task had to be completed so they could make profits off sales for the family's pocket and they could feed on the residue. This was not so much of a rosy income as it could barely settle the family's bills or debts.

In the process of fishing on a sunny afternoon, Stevens took a break because of the heat while he had a conversation with his Dad which was a bit different from the regular casual ones he had in the past just as his uncle, Sam had just come in from Ikeja after a stressful week with some clients. They laughed and talked as this was their recreation but this was a bit different for Stevens as he was fascinated by the way his uncle went around things that were different from his papa. His uncle was more fluent in speaking English than his dad who most times spoke Yoruba or pidgin. They spoke about their passion Stevens made it clear to be marketing as he would consistently follow his mother and top sales.

After a few weeks, his uncle made arrangements for him to get back to school, but this time, with him where he provided a Computer, Internet access, and a smartphone for Stevens to get equipped with some digital skills.

Stevens developed himself with that opportunity and now is a Professional

Writer and Marketer. He provides online services for people like you and me which is called freelancing. He didn't relent due to his background, colour, or race but had the mindset of self-development. Now he makes comfortably $5000- $15000 a month.

Looking at the qualities of Stevens, he was open-minded, broken (had a quest for knowledge), hardworking, and relentless. The risks he took were not portrayed here but I guess you'll get to know meeting him at the top. His inquisitiveness played a unique role in his life.

Now see yourself making those figures and think of an answer to this question, 'Are you putting in the work?', 'Can you commit two hours daily?', 'Do you have a working smartphone/ computer?' because I'm not a money-making guru but I've stumbled on something really good and legitimate and would only like to tell interested and inspired people about it.

The applications of writing are Freelancing, Copywriting, Marketing, IT, and many others. You could even get a raise at work for an additional skillset as this is a high-income skill as you see and this in your toolbox can fetch you a lot. Must read: The Foreign Copywriting Initiative (class of 2022), this is essential to your journey in writing.

If you're a Writer or Content Creator, Read This!

Do you struggle with creating content and putting out value,

Do you run out of ideas while creating content, or writing,

Here's what it took me months to understand and this should help you.

The best writing/ Content ideas come from actually living life and going outside

Time away from writing/ Creating content is where the inspiration comes from.

Also,

Any Social media where you can place a clickable link can be monetized

Hold on to this.

I will discuss another form of generating income on the internet. Now, if you notice, the two opportunities I mentioned above, include step-by-step processes and external links directing you to courses written by successful people who influence one niche or the other. Now what I want to show you is a method of Making money by Affiliating on Hotforex.

Chapter 2

AMAZON KDP BLUEPRINT: MAKE MONEY MONTHLY BY UPLOADING WORD DOCUMENTS TO AMAZON, WITHOUT WRITING A WORD

Earning in dollars and converting back to Naira has always been the dream due to the high exchange rates that are climbing daily. Therefore, to beat inflation, one has to be on the positive side of these crises rather than on the losing side. As of 2009 one dollar was worth about 150-200 naira but now one dollar equals roughly 650, Whereas, Wages aren't increased, and salaries aren't paid consistently.

At this point, one would know making money is better off on the internet remotely and I am about to show you another business model that is in the system for years.

Ps: They won't teach you this in schools because even your lecturers have no idea about the positive side of crises. Follow me closely.

This is introductory, and I will explain the basics things you need to know about Amazon KDP, and why you should get started.

Also if you're already working Your salary is not enough, you are simply working from pocket to mouth.

"I'm going to show you how ordinary people like you are making hundreds, thousands, and hundreds of thousands off Amazon every Month. Like all the classes, workshops, and webinars that I do hold, I only need one serious person who is unhappy about his or her financial situation and is finally ready to make a change, and add a good stream of income for him/her herself.

You can start your journey to gain financial stability by also learning about this amazing business that is currently paying me an average of $1-2K monthly even if you have no experience or digital skills..."

What is Amazon KDP?
Amazon KDP (Kindle Direct Publishing) allows you to
self-publish eBooks, paperbacks, and hardcover books for
free. It gives direct access to your book on Amazon and allows you to create a product detail page for your book.
It also gives you the option to expand your book's availability on a global scale, making it more accessible to readers around the world. Publishing with KDP gives you full rights to your book, which is not something a traditional publishing house typically allows.

Types of content you can publish?

KDP allows you to publish e-books and paperback books. However, KDP does not allow the creation of magazines, periodicals, or spiral-bound books.

You are probably saying you are not a writer, and can't do this, Then this is the catch.

You don't need to write a thing!!

Content types typically published using KDP include but are not limited to the following:

1. Novels
2. Book Series
3. Children's Books
4. Comics
5. Cookbooks
6. Journals
7. Poetry
8. Textbooks

In 2019, authors earned more than $300 million from the Direct Publishing (KDP) Select Global Fund, totalling more than $1.1 billion since the launch of Kindle Unlimited

Since Kindle Unlimited launched, Amazon said, KDP
authors have earned more than $1.1 billion through the
program and more than 1,000 had royalties of $100,000
through KDP in 2019.
You know what KDP is right now, and the potential it holds for you as a writer, we will discuss the steps of publishing...
As we all know, this platform doesn't take Nigerians, but Nigerians have been silently making hundreds of thousands from it. I keep saying that not all the big boys driving Benz around and spending money for their good are fraudsters, there is serious money on the internet...

What are the steps and important aspects of Amazon KDP in publishing a book?

- Set up a KDP account

Publishing on Amazon means that you will need an account to start. One of the mistakes people make is registering the account the wrong way, only to be banned by Amazon, months later. Knowing how to do this sets you up for success or failure.

- Create a new title

On your KDP dashboard, you'll see right away that there's a section called "Create a new title," with two options underneath: Kindle eBook, or Paperback. For this class, we're only going to cover setting up an ebook, though the process for paperbacks (paperback is simply the hard cover part of your book, Amazon handles the printing and shipping of those books to your readers, so you don't need to do anything extra) is pretty similar.

- Enter your book description

The rest of this first tab is where you fill in all the information about your book. This will include, among other details:

- if it's part of a series (you can choose to write books in parts, and keep selling them in small chunks); - the recommended age range of your readers, and any additional contributors who worked on your book, such as a book illustrator.

A bold headline statement, hook, or social validation (if you are well-known or a best seller), is a common approach used by bestselling traditionally published books — there's no reason not to imitate them

- **Select your keywords and categories**

This can be stressful as it is a very important aspect of the process. If you play or don't take this part seriously, it'll drastically affect how much your book sells in a day, a month or if it would be dusted every time someone wants to make a purchase

You have to research for the keywords people essentially for when they come looking for a book related to yours, a lot of the research has to be done by hand.

Clicking through the Kindle store and digging up the data on successful books similar to yours is the best way to find the keywords and categories that feel like a perfect fit. Some tools make it very easy to make this research right on Amazon. And all these tools are free to utilize and available for both laptops, and smartphones (androids only at the moment)
- Upload your written book

The next tab you reach is where you'll need to upload your book onto your KDP account. To get started, simply click the friendly, yellow "Upload ebook manuscript" button. Select the final copy of your book and click "OK."

Amazon will accept a range of file formats, but we strongly recommend having your file formatted as an epub. There is a tool as well where you write in, it will both format, and give you the recommended document format for your kindle book.

If you are using a laptop or smartphone, there are methods you use in writing your book/kindle without writing a single word of your own (you'll use my secret writing strategy that many others are using, and generating a lot of money), and you also see methods of formatting your Kindle the right way.

Because if you ignore all these steps and formats, Amazon will reject your book, and if they mistakenly accept it, it'll get bad reviews, which can lead them to ban you from the platform.

- **Upload a jpeg or tiff version of your cover**

A book won't sell without an attractive cover. Amazon is very strict with cover design dimensions, and you'll get frustrated if they keep moving your book from review mode to draft, needing your attention again. Amazon generally would like a 6" x 9" cover dimension, and this also goes for your Paper back design.

Knowing how important this is, I dedicated a good time using both a laptop and mobile

phone to show you how you can model designs of successful books in your niche, and how you can easily make these designs with your smartphone, and in minutes. Just like uploading your manuscript (your written book), it will take a minute or two to be uploaded and processed, and once completed, you'll receive a green notification about the completion.
Amazon also pays you when 1 out of 300m+ active users read each page of the book.

- Publishing

When you have all these things right, you are faced with publishing your book, and just a click away from reaching the intended audience. Once done, Amazon will review the contents, the covers, categories, and other important things that could affect the reader's experience like formatting before approving your book for publishing.

Advantages of Amazon KDP
- **Ease**

KDP makes self-publishing easy. They've provided detailed documentation, how-to videos, FAQs, forums, and a help centre, all of which can help you understand your self-publishing options. Whether you're new or experienced, you'll be able to use Amazon's self-publishing services easily.

- **Accessibility**

Self-publishing truly opens up the elusive publishing world to new writers. Having free self-publishing options can make that writing dream become a reality for people who may have thought it was impossible. Self-publishing can sometimes be a pricey option, so having an affordable and feasible option for writers is truly groundbreaking.

- Flexibility

In the current world of publishing, writers now have to consider what type of medium they would like to produce – digital or printed. Amazon self-publishing is flexible: you can publish strictly in a digital format (an eBook), you can publish in a paperback, or you can sell your book in both media. The choice is yours!

Pricing

KDP allows authors the option to set the book's pricing. There are some restrictions, though. For example, if you select the 70% royalty program, then the maximum price that your eBook can be sold at is $9.99 in all applicable markets. Be sure to read through the fine print carefully while considering the pros and cons of self-publishing on Amazon.

- Royalties (this is the money you earn from your books on Amazon)

KDP lets you set your royalty plans, giving authors a greater amount of control over their financing. There are two options to choose from: a 35% royalty plan or a 70% royalty plan. You must do your research to figure out which option is best for you.

For example, with the 70% royalty plan, you do need to account for printing and delivery costs, while with the 35% royalty plan, you don't need to account for those fees.

Payment options

Last but not least, Amazon gives reliable payments to authors. Authors are paid every month, but with a 60-day window. So, If you make $100 in August, you won't receive that $100 until October.

This payment gap is notably large for the publishing industry and something to consider when weighing the self-publishing pros and cons.

Though this is simple, it can be tedious if you don't know what to do, and the right tools to use.

Even if you are not a writer, or someone like me who doesn't have much time to spare, but want to build a stream from this pool of dollars, you can still publish at least 3 - 4 books in a week, using my secret writing method.

Before publishing, you need to know the profitable niche, and where you can publish books to make sales, this is important cos it affects how many books you can sell. If you know the right way to do this, it can be easy to do.

I'm sure anxiety is kicking in a bit, ready to hop on? I have an offer for you. There is a **COMPLETE AMAZON KINDLE BLUEPRINT** that you can enrol in today, and start implementing immediately.

There are testimonies of daily, weekly, and monthly earnings of people from this model of making dollars. See Testimonies Here
" I made it so easy that **even a 12 year will understand,** and they are all video tutorials where you'll be peeking over my shoulders while I show you all that you need to start averaging $100 - $500 as a beginner. With more books, profitable niche publishing, and other things you'll learn, **you can start making $500 - $5k monthly in royalties."**

This full course also comes with a community of publishers who are also ready to provide support, assistance, and mentorship
  mentorship at no extra cost.

Some other things you will gain from this blueprint:
1. Detailed description of Amazon KDP is
2. How to create your dollar account
3. How to properly set up your account (even if your
country is banned)
4. How to make book research
5. How to detect a profitable niche
6. How to generate insights for your book
7. How to write without writing a word
8. How to properly set up your account for the success
9. How to withdraw your earned dollars into your country's local bank
10. How to properly price your book and sell like crazy
11. How to design a selling book cover

12. How to list your book in ten categories
13. How to engage with the Amazon help desk
14. How to properly format your book
15. Secrets to selling more books
16. Free tools to use to make things easier for you
17. PRO Canva account for free

Unbelievable yeah? Hop on this Opportunity Now and Early. <u>Click here.</u>

Don't sleep on this, people you are smarter than are silently earning thousands of dollars monthly.

Congratulations for using your time wisely to learn about a new model, You are gradually developing your mind and thoughts by reading through the business models in this book. By the time you are done, all you need is just one business model suitable for you.

Contact me as soon as you hop on this opportunity so I put you through and deliver the support I have promised.

Chapter 3

HOW I MADE $100 IN LESS THAN A MONTH BY AFFILIATING ON HOTFOREX

I want to show you how to take advantage of this opportunity to generate a lot of money for yourself using Hotforex.

Imagine a world where everything is free and you need little or no work at all to purchase and buy the comfort and luxury of this life. In this case, you do not have to worry about bills, commitments, and all that.

Crazy yeah? but Nah, I must say, that's a delusion, it can never happen, but I can show you what can give you a taste of that life without stress.

Now before you run to Google, you can as well ask me, Hotforex is a broker which offers trading services and facilities to both retail and institutional clients. HotForex is **an award-winning forex and commodities broker.** You would also want to know what a broker is but I think you should see the question as 'Who is a broker'

A broker is a person who buys and sells goods or assets for others. In this context, we are looking at a forex broker.

A forex broker is a financial services company that provides traders access to a platform for buying and selling foreign currencies. 'Forex' is an acronym for **foreign exchange**. Transactions in the forex market are always between a pair of two different currencies. Now, hearing FOREX! does it ring a bell? you see or listen to it as scams, but truth is, There's always going to be talks and bias on everything that's out there but you're the one who chooses to take in the chaff or the actual information. What I'm about to show you is a system where you can make money from

Forex whether you know its markets or not. Meaning you do not need any trading experience or do too much but you can comfortably sit at your comfort and make passive income from hotforex by doing what I'm about to show you.

Affiliating with hotforex is simply registering traders on hotforex and these traders who you registered will be your money-making machine.

Simple right? now let us go a bit deeper and explain some terms.

"Money-making machine" doesn't mean these people will work tirelessly for you and you'll just sit in a corner and be enjoying their money, No!

There is so much money in the Forex market and this money is sufficient to go around for all of us.

The market cap for the forex industry is 5.1 trillion dollars DAILY. Yes, I said daily and that's no cap.

So Hotforex pays you for simply registering clients and traders with them. Now your next question is 'How much am I getting paid' but relax and stick with me because I will answer all your questions in this article.

As an affiliate, you're paid a certain percentage of the pips your clients puts in the market, and this happens whether they are on the losing or winning ends. Now let's simplify this, Pip is an acronym for "percentage in point" or **"price interest point."** A pip is the smallest price move that an exchange rate can make based on the forex market convention. Most currency pairs are priced out to four decimal places and the pip change is the last (fourth) decimal point. This isn't as complex as it may sound so if you don't still don't understand this, let me give you my lay-mans explanation. A pip is the forex money so since we have many pairs such as USD, meaning United States Dollar, and GBP meaning Great Britain Pounds the movements in the market on various pairs can only be calculated by having a Standard Convertible Unit such as (S.I Unit).

This unit, pip, can be converted to currency and converted back to pip. I hope you understand this and this doesn't complicate it.

So after your clients have opened their orders, the stipulated percentage which is your commission is paid to you and could be withdrawn.

Wow Wow Wow, sounds crazy right and simple right? Now let us move forward.

HOW TO TAKE ADVANTAGE OF THIS OPPORTUNITY

You dive into this opportunity by setting up a Hotforex account, Talk to Forex traders you know around you that use a different broker, and tell them about the numerous benefits and offers that hotforex offers that their broker might not or isn't offering such as:

- Zero Spreads
- Zero Dollar fees on deposits
- 100% bonus offerings
- 1200+ Trading Instruments
- 1:1000 account Leverage

Help them set up their account by giving them your unique hotforex affiliate link and explaining to them how to verify it which they might know already. This is simply done by submitting your KYC documents and you would be verified. Once they fund their account and start trading, you start making money! Boom! so easy.

HOW TO SET UP YOUR ACCOUNT

This is the most important and fun part of this article because you have to pay attention to details. The first thing you have to do is [click here](.) and fill in the details.

If you aren't able to click it, copy and paste it into your browser and go.

After filling in your details, click on register and confirm your Email address. When all these steps are completed, you have to verify your account by submitting the KYC documents I mentioned earlier. Take a clear photo or

scan the document and can be uploaded on the site or sent via email to the address provided for verification.

Upon completion of this step, you should get a verification message about your success.

Now you go to partners and get your affiliate link.

Every time an account is created, you will be notified via email, and every time you're due for withdrawal which is every Wednesday, you will receive instant payment.

Hello??!! You're still here? I want to show you the most mind-blowing part of this right now, Do you know you can make money off trading off your accounts by simply registering your second my area (that is your second profile which can be in another currency) under your first one and trade on the second one. This means your affiliating your second account thereby making money off your trades. This works perfectly if you're a trader. What are you still waiting for? Use this link and sign up

.

Ps: Creation of an account for this opportunity is free and easy. You do not need any start-up capital to do this business. What you should do is look for those of your rich, consistent forex traders, and encourage them to switch their brokers and start using HotForex. Register them and make sure their account is verified. The moment they start trading, your account gets fatter.

After verification, you have access to my Financial Analysis Telegram channel where I drop Forex Technical analysis.

So look at this, do you feel it is a very legit and suitable way to generate passive income? If yes, I demand you take this opportunity seriously.

Well well, as this is getting hotter line by line, I want to introduce you to the Baba of Long-term investment. This is for the Big boys who have made lots of money and have enough to invest long-term. If you find yourself in this category, Then you should continue. If not, then you should go for one of the above. The one I recommend for those who have zero start-up capital to buy any course is to affiliate with Hotforex I have mentioned above.

Now, we shall continue to the next opportunity which is Cryptocurrency.

Now, this is a very volatile business opportunity which means that in the same way it can make you very rich within two days, it can send you back to the village that fast too. That is why this is recommended for the Big boys who are ready to go long-term and ready to play by its rules.

Chapter 4

Cryptocurrency, the new oil well? Catch the flight!

For the first time in the history of mankind, anyone with a phone and an internet connection now has the "key" and can join Billionaires like Elon Musk, Bill Gates, and Mark Cuban, to Multiply Money in what Forbes Magazine calls "The Greatest Wealth Transfer of All Time".

The Letter Below Is About How You Can Safely Use Bitcoin and Other Smaller Crypto Coins to Multiply Your

Money In 2022… Even If You Don't Know What a "Coin" Means

Plus Access to a Sacred List of 10 Crypto Coins That Could Produce 50–100x Returns.

Having a group of knowledgeable friends around you that have vast knowledge in the crypto markets and can put you through could be a blessing but at this point being exposed to professional experience in the crypto markets from what I'm about to show you is Divine. This expertise shows you detailed procedures for moving from the Beginner level to a greater yield.

An EPIC movement and transfer of wealth are happening right now in the world and for the first time in recorded human history, anyone can participate...

"...No Matter the Colour of Your Skin, the Language You Speak, Your Nationality, or Even How Much Money You Currently Have..."

You might be thinking about it being too late to invest in Bitcoin but this is more of finding and doing your research on purposeful coins that will hit the market and give you great ROI (meaning Return on Investment).

This teaches you how to study them, what signs to look out for, and find them out early and this can make you extremely rich.

As you likely already know, there are other coins, hundreds of them in fact, created to address different target markets and different business sectors.

Now, there are practically cryptocurrencies for gamers, for the energy market, for the financial market, for the law/contract/compliance sectors, for AI (artificial intelligence), and so on.

And these coins, in many cases have generated more than 100,000% ROI!

Coins like:

- Binance Coin (BNB) has returned gains of 430,779.75% ROI

- Ethereum (ETH) which has returned gains of 279,843% ROI

- Ripple (XRP) which has returned gains of 36,000% ROI

- Litecoin (LTC) which has returned gains of 5,100% ROI

And many more coins doing incredible returns.

But the KEY Is In...Finding and Buying Them Early...

Cryptocurrencies are knitted into the fabric of this world as this can be seen as Bitcoin and other crypto assets have been legalized by the US government and the race to enter the market is very fast. Companies like Paypal and Visa have incorporated the ability to make and receive payments via Bitcoin among their offered services.

In other words, Bitcoin and cryptocurrency are here to stay.

I mean... everybody and their friends are jumping in to collect their share,

Why Not You Too?

But as I previously mentioned, most people don't know how it works, or that you can buy fractions of Bitcoin or any cryptocurrency you want.

TRUTH:

They don't know where to buy it or keep it safe, and they don't know WHEN to buy and WHEN to sell.

What's worse is most new people are investing too much money into Bitcoin, at the wrong time, or selecting the wrong coins, then generating monumental losses and crying about how everyone else is getting rich except them.

The worst thing you could do is invest money in Bitcoin and crypto assets while trying to figure everything out on your own.

Bitcoin and crypto-assets can be volatile, and you should never invest more money than you can afford to.

But what is even more important is for you to know how much to safely and responsibly invest into crypto when to do so, and when to sell, because this is the critical information that anyone who wants to invest in crypto needs to have, if they desire to create wealth.

And to help do it, I am presenting you the ***Cryptocurrency Wealth Builders Blueprint***

The Cryptocurrency Wealth Builders Blueprint is a set of step-by-step instructional videos that breaks down everything you need to know about Bitcoin and other cryptocurrencies — what it is, how to buy, when to buy, how to secure it, and when to sell it — everything. This is a must-read and you should [check this out now!!](#).

You have come to the end of this E-book. Take this information seriously. You are always free to contact me via my socials if you need any form of help or answers to questions. **Bless**.

www.ingramcontent.com/pod-product-compliance
Lightning Source LLC
Chambersburg PA
CBHW070317220526
45465CB00004B/1890